CHRISTIAN SPIRITUALITY

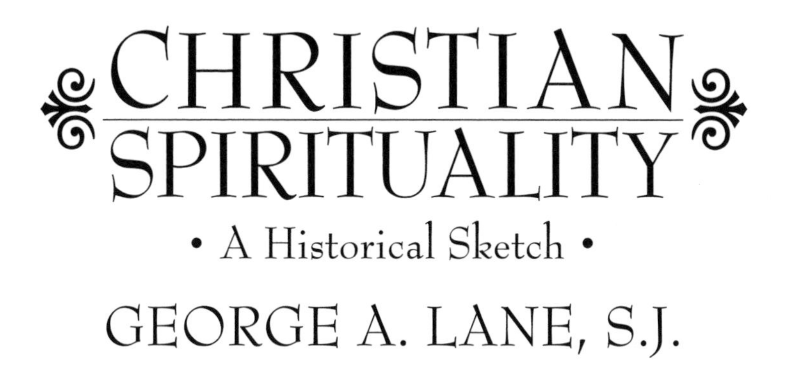

LOYOLAPRESS.
CHICAGO

LOYOLAPRESS.
3441 N. ASHLAND AVENUE
CHICAGO, ILLINOIS 60657
(800) 621-1008
WWW.LOYOLABOOKS.ORG

The materials in this book—originally presented in the form of lectures by Thomas M. Gannon, S.J., George W. Traub, S.J., and George A. Lane, S.J.—were rewritten for publication by George A. Lane and were first published in booklet form by Argus Communications Co.

The present edition is a Loyola Request Reprint. It is reprinted by arrangement with the author and/or the original publisher and is now sold only by Loyola Press.

Portions of this book appear in revised and amplified form in *The Desert and the City* by Thomas M. Gannon and George W. Traub.

Library of Congress Cataloging-in-Publication Data

Lane, George, 1934-
Christian spirituality : a historical sketch / George A. Lane.
p. cm.
Originally published: Chicago : Loyola University Press, c1984.
Includes bibliographical references.
ISBN 0-8294-2081-9
1. Spirituality—Catholic Church—History. 2. Catholic Church—Doctrines—History. I. Title.
BX2350.65.L36 2004
248'.088'282—dc22

2004008517

Printed in the United States of America
04 05 06 07 08 09 10 Bang 10 9 8 7 6 5 4 3 2 1

Contents

Introduction vii

Protest and Renunciation in the East 1

The Ideal of Contemplation 9

Benedictine Spirituality 17

The Mendicant Transition 25

The Religious Climate of the Later Middle Ages 31

The Nature of Mysticism 37

Ignatian Prayer: Finding God in All Things 43

The Contemplative Climate in Sixteenth-Century Spain 51

Ignatian Prayer, Second Generation 55

Finding God's Will: Discernment 63

Spirituality for Our Time 71

Notes 81

Introduction

In the years since the Second Vatican Council, the church has taken a new and multifaceted interest in spirituality, particularly in spirituality's psychological aspects. Much of this interest has been directed toward an understanding of the unique individual human person who seriously tries to live a spiritual life. This psychological dimension has ushered in a much more humane approach to many aspects of spirituality, which was much needed to counter the ultramechanical piety of the nineteenth and early twentieth centuries. There has also been a fruitful theological dimension to this spiritual renewal. Recent decades have seen a wealth of theological insight into matters of the spiritual life, providing a rich vein of reflection that has immeasurably deepened contemporary spirituality.

The chief problem confronting any kind of renewal, especially renewal of the spiritual life, is to balance the changing with the changeless, the demands of contemporaneity with the treasures of the past. How to find this balance is the problem we face in attempting to formulate a spirituality that is at once vital for our time and yet solidly grounded in the best traditions of the historical church.

My interest in this book is in the second of these demands—an understanding of Christian tradition. I propose to make a historical-theological survey of Christian spirituality with the hope that this book can help readers base their spiritual renewal on the firm ground of the Christian tradition. As in so much of the work of Vatican II, we look to the sources of Christian life and try to discover how Christianity has developed. As Pierre Teilhard de Chardin said, "Everything is the sum of the past; nothing is comprehensible except through its history."[1] And similarly, a failure to grasp the historical perspective so often condemns people to relive the mistakes of the past. To arrive at an authentic program for seeking union with God in our present time, we keep both the past and the future in mind. We must preserve the best traditions from the past and look to the future for our goals.

In a broad sense, spirituality may be described as a way to holiness. More precisely, spirituality is humanity's possession by God in Christ through the Holy Spirit. In a sense, there is only one Christian spirituality because there is only one Christ. However, when the means of union with God become concretized, various styles of approach to this union appear. Any particular style of approach to union with God can properly be called a spirituality. As John Courtney Murray, S.J., said, God would have each person wholly to be his witness, but not necessarily a witness to the whole of him. Only the church, as the community of the faithful, can really bear witness to the whole counsel of God in many-splendored variety.[2]

Indeed, we see many approaches to spirituality throughout Christian history. Society challenges each man and woman differently, and these challenges call forth different responses to God. Some of these responses by extraordinary men and women—the hermits of the East, the monks of the West, Basil, Athanasius, Origen, Jerome, Augustine, Benedict, Dominic, Francis, Teresa of Ávila, Catherine of Siena, Ignatius, and Thérèse of Lisieux are among the best known—were so penetrating that large numbers of Christians followed them. Their influence and their insights live on.

As we will see in this book, there is a distinction between the basic worldview (or God-view) of these great men and women and certain techniques used by their followers to implement the vision. The vision is unchangeable, but the techniques used to implement and institutionalize it are intrinsically and necessarily adaptive.

We will also see how certain structural elements remain constant throughout the history of Christian spirituality. Although they may be implemented differently at different times, an authentically Christian spirituality must provide for such perennial elements as prayer, penance, mortification, and apostolic activity. This has always been true, and it is true today.

There is much talk today of finding a contemporary spirituality by searching the writings of our own contemporary artists and thinkers. This will undoubtedly be helpful, but we will find an authentic spirituality only by probing the mystery of Christ as he is transmitted to us through the history of the believing church. Accordingly, our effort will be to distinguish between the vision of the great leaders in the church and certain intrinsically adaptive techniques, and to try to fit the enduring values to the spirit and conditions of our own time.

A final word of caution. As we survey the history of Christian spirituality, we need to keep in mind a distinction between a systematic understanding of a spirituality and the lived experience of the spirituality. Ideally they should coincide and infuse each other. But the reality is that the lived experiences of the great founders of religious orders is a unique thing, and it dies out with the people who have had that experience. It is not the lived experience that influences us but rather the theology of it. The way that experience was explained and interpreted survives. For example, some of the problems we might have about the spirituality of the early desert hermits in the East were not necessarily problems for them, but they are for us. We do not have their experience; we do have the systematic explanation of their way of life, and this is what influences us. We cannot criticize their life experience; but we can criticize and evaluate their articulation or explanation of it in order to discover what may be valid for our own purposes.

Protest and Renunciation in the East

In the centuries after Christ, many Christians led lives of self-denial, prayer, fasting, and celibacy in imitation of Jesus. Most did so in their towns, in the midst of their families. However, toward the beginning of the fourth century, significant numbers of men and women in the East began to withdraw from the world and lead lives of self-denial in the desert. By the end of the fourth century, thousands of monks and nuns were living in the wastelands of the interior of Egypt, as well as in desolate spots in Syria and Palestine. Some lived as cenobites (persons living together in community), but many others lived solitary lives. All subsequent monastic movements are rooted in this early flight to the desert of Egypt, and "Eastern monasticism" has had a lasting impact on the development of spirituality.

The Eastern monastic movement is difficult for us to understand because we are far removed in time from the monks of the desert. These early monks inflicted severe physical and psychological deprivations on themselves. Most of us would regard these penances as extreme and hardly worthy of imitation today. We have many more models for leading a holy life than they had.

Yet it is not altogether impossible to appreciate why people might want to flee from the world into the quiet sandy desert to come into contact with God. To approach the Eastern monastic movement, as well as the whole of spirituality, we have to recognize a certain basic yearning for self-surrender that is present in every person. This yearning rises at times to a passion; it is something of an instinct that we cannot fully explain. It is a drive that leads many people, almost in spite of themselves, to moments of heroic decision to give their lives to others. There are few people who do not, on occasion, have a vision of a nobler life and a better existence. We seek an escape from a restrictive and repressive conscience, we yearn for the infinite, we search for meaning, we desire God.

This yearning for self-surrender is a given with the human situation, the basic presupposition to which Christ appeals in the Gospels. For those who accept Christ as the Lord and commit themselves entirely to him, this self-surrender is an imperative call of the Master. "Whoever loves father or mother more than me is not worthy of me. . . . And whoever does not take up the cross and follow me is not worthy of me"(Mt. 10:37–38). We can understand passages like this in the New Testament if we see them in the light of the church and in the history of the people who have done this sort of thing.

This desire to follow Christ is what was underneath the Eastern monastic response. The form of this surrender has changed through the years, but its starting point has always been the same, an acceptance of and a commitment to the risen

Lord. As they read the Gospel, the people who became the monks of the desert believed wholeheartedly that the only way to respond authentically to Christ was to get away from the din of the world and to go out to the desert to find him there. One had to flee the city of sin in order to find God, the pure God who was wholly other, wholly apart, and wholly transcendent to this city of sinful humanity.

Unfortunately some of the heroic austerities of the monks often overshadowed the real essence of their life and work. Coupled with certain unusual practices was a desire for protest and renunciation that permeated the entire Eastern movement. These men felt the world was evil. The only way they could achieve union with Christ was to protest the evil world and renounce these evil temptations.

Along with this desire in the Eastern monastic movement was a captivating enthusiasm. These men were utterly convinced that theirs was a magnificent vocation. They did not condemn others but looked upon them as hopelessly caught in the turmoil of the world. The monks felt that they had made a great discovery, finding the only way to profound union with God. This enthusiasm comes out in St. Athanasius's life of St. Anthony the Hermit, which is one of the many stories of the desert monks that inspired Christians at the time, and which continue to do so today. Anthony had lived forty years in the desert, and when people went out to visit him

> [h]e came forth as from some shrine, like one who has been initiated in the sacred mysteries, and filled with the spirit of God. Then, for the first time, he was seen outside the fort by those who came to him. They were amazed to

> see that his body was unchanged, for it had not become heavy from lack of exercise, nor worn from fasting and struggling with the evil spirits; he was just as they had known him before he had secluded himself. The temper of his soul, too, was faultless, for it was neither straightened as if from grief, nor dissipated by pleasure, nor was it strained by laughter or melancholy. He was not disturbed when he saw the crowd, nor elated at being welcomed by such large numbers; he was perfectly calm, as befits a man who is guided by reason and who has remained in his natural state. (The state in which Adam and Eve were created, but which was damaged by the fall.) Through him the Lord healed many of those who were suffering in body and freed them from evil spirits.[3]

This type of response to the Gospel seems more intelligible—and even necessary—against the background of the times. In its earliest days, the Roman authorities treated the young church with tolerance because it was viewed as a Jewish sect. But soon tolerance diminished and the authorities began to view Christians as an alien group that made trouble with its disdain for the gods of the state. Persecution followed and, for Christians, martyrdom became the pinnacle of Christian renunciation. It was a way in which a man or woman could say, "I am renouncing myself, taking up my cross, and literally following Christ."

When the period of martyrdom and persecutions was over, people needed another way to reach the pinnacle of Christian perfection. Martyrdom had been the ideal, and now there were no martyrs. The notion of rejecting the world and surrendering to God in a life of privation in the desert became an alternative to martyrdom. Indeed, writings of the period show that the monks of the desert did view going into hermitage as another way to reach the height of perfection previously achieved by martyrdom. In addition, the character of the church changed when Emperor Constantine embraced Christianity in AD 313. Many new people became Christian and, in the process, diluted the original "quality." Fervent Christians who had withstood persecution were joined by power seekers and half-converted pagans. Understandably, longtime Christians were unhappy.

Monasticism was a protest against this dilution. It was a protest not just against the world, but especially against the world in the church. It's important to understand that monasticism was originally a lay movement. In fact, the monks were quite anticlerical in a prophetic sense, similar to the anticlericalism of such Jewish prophets as Amos and Hosea, who condemned those priests who did not preach justice and love but became fully enmeshed in the power structure of the state. Accordingly, the monastic movement should be seen not so much within the church as alongside it.

Many of these early monks firmly believed that God could not be found among men. One story makes the point well. Abbot Marcus asked the Abbot Arsenius, "'Wherefore do you flee from us?'; and the old man said, 'God knows that I love you, but I cannot be with God and with men—a thousand and a thousand thousand angelic powers have one will, but men have many. Therefore I cannot send God from me and come and be with men.'"[4]

The corrupt and corroding city of man was another factor that prompted the withdrawal to the city of God in the desert.

The empire was decaying; nothing seemed able to reverse the unraveling of organized society. Withdrawal from society seemed quite attractive, even wise.

The monastic movement evolved gradually. The early monks lived in cities and went out into the desert later on as part of an intensifying desire to flee the world. At first, individuals went out alone to solitary hermitages, but most gradually banded together for survival's sake and to better support one another in their demanding lives. Nevertheless, solitary living was common.

The ideals of monasticism are still operative today. Dom Hubert Van Zeller points out that it is "not in outward activities that the strength of monasticism lies. The direct contribution is not and never has been the main thing. The main thing has been the indirect contribution made by prayer and penance . . . the monk who loves God perfectly is fulfilling every obligation, which in Christian charity he owes to his neighbor."[5]

There is always need for renunciation and solitude in the spiritual life. The question that we must ask is What forms should protest, renunciation, and solitude take today?

As a movement that involved relatively few people, early Eastern monasticism seems elitist to us. The monks seemed to be a breed set apart in favored conditions in an isolated environment. Does Christ preach an elitist spirituality in the Gospel? It seems not. There is also the problem of what we might call the essentialist view of human nature—the notion that human beings are made up of distinct component parts with mind and spirit warring against the flesh. One might go off to the desert to fight oneself, to conquer the flesh definitively, but such a person will usually find that he is his own worst enemy. He creates more problems in isolation than he ever would have found in contact with other people. Not only does he run the risk of exposing himself to greater conflict than he would have found among people, but the problems will have been of his own making. And then in face of the social difficulties of the time, perhaps it was easier to abandon the sinking ship of the church rather than try to guide it into port.

The contemporary question that we must ask ourselves is how can we preserve the ideals of protest and renunciation of this way of life while sifting out the ideals and customs that have come down to us and that are not suited to our age or mentality?

The Ideal of Contemplation

As Christianity spread throughout the Greco-Roman world in the first centuries after Christ, it came into contact with the prevailing pagan philosophies of the time—most notably, that of Plato. Plato taught that matter and spirit are sharply divided. Material things are merely temporal manifestations of eternal forms or ideas. These immutable forms are the true ground of reality, the proper subject of philosophical contemplation. Another philosophical school with great influence in the pagan world was Stoicism. The Stoics were especially known for their ethical idea of *apatheia,* which held that human beings should strive to achieve a state of detachment from irrational passions.

These Greek philosophical ideas shaped the ethical and moral thinking of the pagan world that the Christians encountered in the early centuries of the church. Christian leaders and teachers found themselves in conversation with educated pagans who were schooled in philosophical dualism—spirit in opposition to matter. They believed that a spiritual human soul emanates from a supreme intelligence, the One, and is imprisoned in the material, evil body. This imprisonment of the soul accounts for all the evil in the world. The spiritual challenge was to become a true ascetic, to fight one's body, overcome it, and strive to reach a state of *apatheia*—insensitivity to all things of this world. The serious Greek-educated spiritual seeker of the time was involved in a struggle to bring the flesh under control. His principal task was to allow the soul to escape, release itself, and reascend to its place of origin in the One. The serious seeker strove to achieve a state of *gnosis*. Here, the soul achieves total freedom from the body and fixes its attention solely on spiritual realities. The mind contemplates the One and thereby anticipates its state of reabsorption into the One, which is its final destiny. The two processes of this asceticism, *apatheia* and *gnosis,* were both part of the intellectual milieu in third- and fourth-century Alexandria.

Early Christian thinkers in the Greek world attempted to synthesize Christian practice and teaching with these pagan philosophical ideas, drawing what was sound into Christian spirituality and discarding the rest. This effort was centered in the city of Alexandria, in Egypt, and its greatest exponent was the great philosopher Origen (185–254). Origen drew many people around him with his magnetic personality. His life was marked both by great austerities and an immensely energetic devotion to the apostolate. He effected the most successful synthesis of pagan philosophy and Christianity.

Origen's doctrine of Christocentric asceticism and mysticism began by rejecting the pagan view of perfection. Human perfection for him was not to be found in knowledge but in love and the works of charity. For Origen, renunciation, asceticism, and contemplation were not the end of the spiritual life but means for conquering evil inclinations and achieving a perfect love of Christ, who is the actual end and aim of spirituality. Yet Origen valued these ascetical practices and advocated a spirituality in which the person leaves behind corporeal thoughts and images about God and comes to grasp God through pure intellect.

Origen's thought influenced those who fled into the desert about a half century after his death. But when his great Christian synthesis was taken up by the desert monks, it proved too delicate, and it succumbed to the influence of the pagan philosophical milieu, especially in the hands of Evagrius Ponticus (346–399).

Evagrius is a mysterious figure who has had a powerful impact on the development of Christian spirituality. His doctrines were condemned by the Council of Alexandria in 399, but his ideas continued to have influence through Nilus of Ancyra, St. Basil, and other orthodox teachers.

Evagrius was a great enthusiast. He came from Asia Minor near the Black Sea. In his early life he was tried by temptations against chastity, and he fled to the desert near Jerusalem, where there were many thriving monastic communities. He moved on to Egypt, where he spent the last twenty years of his life teaching and writing in the desert outside Alexandria. Evagrius lived until 399, and it was only a few months after his death in that year that his doctrines were condemned.

The doctrine of Evagrius is that of Origen with most of the essentials of Christianity removed. The importance of Evagrius's work lies in the way that he systematized many elements of asceticism as they were preached and practiced in his circles. He laid down rules for what he called the *active life* and the *contemplative life,* though these terms have special meanings in his system and are not to be confused with our contemporary understanding of them.

For Evagrius, the active life is virtue achieved through the analysis and methodical avoidance of vice. Evagrius originated the idea of the "deadly sins." He proposed eight of them—gluttony, fornication, avarice, anger, sadness, listlessness, vainglory, and pride. The methodical ridding of the soul of these vices was carried on in order to achieve the negative goal of *apatheia.* Without this insensitivity to the world it would be impossible for a person to move on to the contemplative life.

One moves to the contemplative stage once perfect control over the body and material things is achieved. In contemplation another kind of asceticism takes hold—that of the mind. The mind is systematically purged of all images, symbols, and concepts so that eventually it reaches a certain unconsciousness, *anaesthesia.* This unconsciousness brings the very highest type of knowledge: knowledge in pure contact with God apart from any human or worldly content. Thus, the object of the contemplative life is to gradually empty the mind in order for God to come in and fill it. This is the very perfection of all Christian and human life.

This concept of contemplation leads to Evagrius's understanding of prayer as a raising of the *mind* to God. Everything is to be sacrificed for the pursuit of prayer. "Go," Evagrius says, "sell all that you have and take up the Cross; deny yourself so that you can pray without distraction."[6] He teaches, "If you would pray worthily, deny yourself continually; if you undergo trials of all sorts, accept your lot philosophically out of love for prayer."[7] Prayer is a chance for the soul to escape, at least temporarily, from the body. Evagrius says, "When your intelligence goes out of the body and rejects all thoughts that come from sense and memory and bodily humors and is filled with awe and joy, then it is allowable to think that you are close to the confines of prayer."[8]

Such prayer is an emptying of the mind, an impassive state of existence free of all feeling and emotion. "Even if the intelligence raises itself above the contemplation of bodily nature, it has not yet perfect contemplation of God because it can still mingle with the intelligibles and share in their multiplicity."[9] In the end, for Evagrius, prayer is an angelic activity. "You wish to pray?" he asks. "Depart from here below and have your dwelling continually on high, not in name only but by a kind of angelic practice and by a knowledge more divine."[10]

The active life and the contemplative life do not intermingle in the doctrine of Evagrius. One goes through a process of purification in the active life and gradually achieves a state of insensitivity. Only then is it possible to pass on to the contemplative life, where prayer becomes an emptying of the mind in order that God may be encountered free from any trace of what is human or worldly. Evagrius made a cult of contemplation. "Pure" prayer and perfection are identified. This prayer—not the love and service of Christ—is the goal of the Christian life.

The two most important transmitters of the Evagrian teaching are John Cassian and an unknown writer known to history as Pseudo-Dionysius. John Cassian was a close associate of Evagrius in the Egyptian desert. Cassian made his way to southern France, where he established religious communities for men and women and wrote two famous works, the *Institutes* and the *Conferences.* In these books Cassian transmitted Evagrius's doctrine to the West in a somewhat tempered form. However, he still held that the ideal of angelic contemplation was the goal and perfection of the Christian life. Anything else, any time taken from contemplation, was taken from God.

The writings of Pseudo-Dionysius emerged in the sixth century. As far as scholars have been able to determine, Pseudo-Dionysius lived around AD 500 and was probably a hermit in the deserts of Syria. Yet the writer of these works, who called himself Dionysius, claimed that he was a confidant of the apostles, that he was present at the crucifixion of Christ, that he was with St. John when the Apocalypse was composed, and that he heard St. Paul make his famous speech in the Areopagus in Athens—all assertions that are obviously wide of the truth. Nevertheless, after St. Augustine, Pseudo-Dionysius is the source most frequently quoted by Thomas Aquinas. This is an indication of the enormous influence he had upon the thinking of the Middle Ages.

Pseudo-Dionysius refined the ideas of Evagrius into techniques. How was one to achieve the ideal of contemplation? The work of Pseudo-Dionysius was an attempt to transfer a "spiritual" ideal into a program of mystical psychology. A negative methodology is the key to the program. One looks at the things of this world and attributes their perfections to God. Any imperfections are not attributed to God. Pseudo-Dionysius transferred this method to the psychological realm. To achieve mystical union with God in contemplation, one goes through a carefully calculated set of steps for gradually bringing the mind under control and emptying it of all its worldly contents.

Because of Dionysius's supposed authority as an intimate of the apostles, his works enjoyed great popularity in the West; and he supplied a vocabulary that would later be used by such mystics as Meister Eckhart and John of the Cross.

The ideas of Origen, Evagrius, and their disciples have had great influence through the centuries. In this spirituality, prayer is the raising of the intelligence above and beyond all things to God. All is to be sacrificed for it. This is the highest of all human activities. To achieve it is to be perfect. It makes man like the angels; it effects heaven on earth. It is clear, however, that this style of prayer is more strongly determined by the Alexandrian philosophical tradition than it is by sacred scripture.

It is also true that this school of spirituality developed apart from the ordinary Christian community. It was developed by people who wanted to separate themselves from the church in protest against it.

Many hard questions arise in connection with this school of spirituality. Should human beings do what angels do? Should we do on earth what we will do in heaven? More fundamentally, is heaven totally different from earth, a kind of pure gazing on the infinite, or are there continuities? Will heaven be a purely intellectual exercise where our bodies (despite the orthodox doctrine of the resurrection of the body) have no place at all? It is perhaps not fair to pass judgment on this movement. At the same time it would be a serious mistake if we uncritically accepted some of these techniques and ideals of spirituality.

We must ask ourselves where our notion of prayer comes from. Is it a bit Evagrian? Does it have to be de-Alexandrianized?

While prayer itself remains an essential of the Christian life, the precise form it takes in any culture must be suited to the mentality of that age, and it must also conform to the Gospel.

Benedictine Spirituality

Our survey of spirituality now shifts from the East to the West as we look at the Benedictine ideal of spirituality. We will find it shaped by a simpler, less sophisticated culture in the West, a more biblical notion of God, and the particular grace and personality of St. Benedict.

Benedict, the founder of Western monasticism, was born in the Italian city of Nursia in Umbria around the year 480, and he lived until 547. In his youth Benedict went to Rome to study but found the city a chaos of disorder and corruption. He left Rome to live a more fervent Christian life. He became a hermit and lived alone on Mt. Subiaco.

After three years of solitude, Benedict, joining with some other monks who gathered around him, made his first attempt at monastic community. Benedict was well acquainted with the disorderly varieties of the monastic life, that were then prevalent both in the East and West. He tried to get his companions to live a fervent monastic life, but his fellow monks did not like the idea; they tried to poison him. Benedict moved on and eventually set up twelve different monasteries around Mt. Subiaco.

Around the year 528, he went to Monte Cassino, founded a monastery, and wrote the Holy Rule in the last years of his life.

Both Eastern and Western monasticism had been plagued by freelance monks who experimented with different ways of life. In the beginning of his Rule, Benedict specifies that he is making a definite break from all that. The Benedictine spiritual ideal is described this way by Cardinal Aiden Gasquet in his commentary on the Holy Rule: "Benedict regarded monastic life . . . as a systematized form of life on the lines of the Gospel counsels of perfection, to be lived for its own sake and as a full expression of the Church's true and perfect life—the perfect liturgical life and that of perfecting the individual soul."[11] Personal sanctification, the Gospel counsels of perfection, and liturgical life in community are the heart of the Benedictine ideal. The goal of the Benedictine way of life is the perfecting of the individual soul through the perfect living of the Christian life in community.

Life in community is essential for Benedict. The apostolate of the monk is entirely indirect. "The monk who loves God perfectly is fulfilling every obligation which in Christian charity he owes to his neighbor."[12]

This love of God is practiced within the monastery, which should then strive to be a perfectly self-sufficient institution. "The monastery, if possible, should be so constructed that all things necessary may be contained within it, water, a mill, a garden, a bakery, and the various workshops, so that there may be no need for the monks to go abroad, for this is not at all healthful for their souls."[13] A direct apostolate of service to the neighbor was not part of the original vision of Benedict.

Many monks of the time lived disorganized and often disorderly lives. To counteract this, Benedict insisted that monastic life be organized according to rule. The Rule would be based on the Bible. The abbot himself was under the Rule, not over it.

Benedict's Rule is characterized by moderation and discretion in all things. A life of controlled simplicity with sufficient food and clothing was noticeably different from the austerities of some of the Eastern monks. The Holy Rule also prescribed the daily order in the monastery; it did not encourage individuality, rather community living with most of the monks doing the same thing at the same time. Everyone rose together and came to the choir together. If someone was late, he had to sit in a special place conspicuous to all.

Stability was another important aspect of the Benedictine life. Monks would make their vows to one monastery and then live out their lives in that same house. This was undoubtedly a response to the social flux and disorder of the times. As a stable institution in an unstable world, the monastery became the locus of faith and learning.

The social structure of the monastic community resembled that of a family. The abbot, the superior, was the father of the community. He held the post for life, thus giving the monastery continuity, stability, unity, and consistency. The monks vowed obedience to the abbot as to Christ. Since the monks thought of themselves as a family, their numbers were restricted to keep the monastery within family proportions. When they grew too numerous, some branched off and started a new community.

The monastery itself was thought of as a home. The vow of stability made it a *personal* stable society—a family that stayed in one place. It is interesting to note that Benedict's Rule is drawn up for one monastery, not for a monastic order. It was only later that the Benedictines were considered an order.

It is important to recall that all the monks were originally laymen. Chapter 62 of the Holy Rule says clearly, "If an abbot desires to have a priest or a deacon ordained for his community, let him choose from among his monks one who is worthy to perform the priestly office."[14] But the priest, if there is to be one in the community, is to have no preference or precedence over anybody else.

Daily life in the monastery consisted of a balance of three elements: liturgical prayer, manual labor, and the prayerful reading of the Bible, called *lectio divina.*

Liturgical prayer is chiefly the chanting of the Divine Office in choir according to the canonical hours. This is an essential element of monastic life, and it is the element that sets the rhythm for the whole monastic life. A good part of Benedict's Holy Rule is devoted to prescriptions as to how the Divine Office is to be sung.

The second integral part of the daily order of the monastery is daily manual labor. The purpose of work was to avoid idleness and to take care of the material needs of the monastery. Manual labor provided necessary physical exercise for the monks. Benedict preferred that the work be farmwork. We note that the work element in Benedictine life was not conceived as apostolic service. It was not intended to serve the needs of the church directly nor was it mission oriented, but it was essentially an element in the balanced daily order for the good of the monks and the community.

The third element in the daily life of a monk was the *lectio divina*—a quiet prayerful reading of sacred Scripture. Says a scholar of monasticism, "To read sacred scripture was in fact to meditate on it and the process could easily turn into prayer, and prayer which could become contemplative; but this would be a gift of God to be waited for and not sought."[15] This, of course, is radically different from the contemplative prayer ideal of Origenism. *Lectio divina* is not trying to be in heaven while still on earth, rather it is a much more realistic type of prayer. Benedict does not use the word "contemplation" anywhere in his Rule. He turned away from John Cassian and others who saw a conscious seeking of the angelic life as the ideal and aim of the spiritual life. For Benedict, perfection is not in tranquillity and contemplation, rather it is in charity, humility, and obedience in community life.

The monastic way of life remains a beautiful and practical ideal of the spiritual life. It has been part of the Christian life for many centuries, since the time of Benedict, and it is lived today in many monasteries throughout the world.

Very early in Benedictine history definite departures were made from the way of life that Benedict laid out in his Rule. These departures from the original concept can be viewed either as a deviation from or a development of the Benedictine way of life.

The first departure came when Pope Gregory the Great called upon the Benedictines to evangelize England. The Benedictines responded and evangelized England and much of northern Europe as well under the leadership of the great

Benedictine saints Augustine of Canterbury, Benet, Bede, Boniface, and many more.

This missionary apostolate called for monks who were also priests. Ultimately, the Benedictines changed from a lay to a predominantly clerical institute. Preparing men for the priesthood introduced teachers, books, learning, libraries, and the whole ideal of study as work in the monastery. The work element in the monastery began to change from farmwork to intellectual work. Schools to train priest-monks eventually accepted outside students and, over time, evolved into the great monastery schools of the Middle Ages. Teaching, study, and manuscript work eventually almost entirely displaced the manual work of the monks. Lay help was secured to work the fields of the monasteries.

Under the missionary demand of the church, the Benedictine spiritual ideal shifted from personal sanctification for the individual to apostolic ministry in the service of the church.

Are these departures from the Benedictine ideal or legitimate developments of it? Benedictines themselves are divided on this question. The answer depends on one's ideas of renewal and on theories of the development of religious traditions.

It will be helpful to briefly consider two major Benedictine reform movements—the Cluniac and the Cistercian reforms of the tenth and twelfth centuries respectively.

The Cluniac reform chiefly concerned certain governmental and liturgical aspects of the Benedictine life and organization. During the feudal age, many monasteries acquired large and valuable land holdings, and their abbots controlled much wealth. This led to abuses and conflict between religious and secular authority. The Cluny reform created a centralized federation of monasteries by affiliating smaller houses with larger ones. Ultimately some fifteen hundred monasteries in western Europe affiliated with Cluny. The effect of this was to free monasteries from secular and episcopal entanglements.

Another important aspect of the Cluny reform was a greatly increased emphasis on the liturgy. Long, elaborate, and magnifi-cently performed liturgical ceremonies were developed. The Divine Office grew beyond what St. Benedict had prescribed, and the prayer element grew to such proportions that it almost eliminated the work element in Benedictine life, and the original balance was lost.

The Cistercian reform began around 1100 and was chiefly an effort to return to the original monastic life as prescribed by St. Benedict. The reformers wanted a literal interpretation of the Holy Rule. This meant removing the additions to the Divine Office that had come in with Cluny; a return to manual labor, preferably farmwork instead of manuscript work or teaching; a return to concern for interior personal sanctification; and a return to solitude, locating the monastery in a remote place. The Cistercian ideal renounced the property, wealth, and power that had come to many of the monasteries, though many Cistercian communities did become prosperous in the Middle Ages.

The spiritual ideal of the Benedictine Rule prizes balance. The Christian life is lived in a regular balanced cycle of meditative reading of the sacred Scripture interspersed with work, with the whole life regulated by the chanting of the Divine Office in choir. The Benedictines consider that any overemphasis or neglect of any of these elements is a departure from the ideal of St. Benedict. Benedictine history shows a certain polarity between reform and renewal that is pertinent today. One pole is the spirit and the words and the writings of the founder. The other pole is the demands of the times and the demands of the church in light of the Holy Spirit. These two interact, always posing the question: how can we find a harmonious balance between the founder's original vision and how it is realized in the world as it is now?

The Mendicant Transition

In the opening years of the thirteenth century, religious life in the church entered upon a great change. Without altering their basic vows of poverty, chastity, and obedience, many of those in religious life sought to work out their ideals by seeking to serve people directly. Up to this time the highest religious life had been identified with a retreat from the world, life in a quiet place far from the noise and bustle, where people could develop virtue and piety and save their souls. But the Franciscan and Dominican friars were different. They were social laborers who went into the world doing good.

Friars who work in this manner are called mendicants, the term referring to members of religious orders who combine an active social apostolate with a refusal to own personal or communal property. What we might call the mendicant transition accompanied a general shift in western Europe from a predominantly rural agrarian culture to an urban commercial culture. Feudalism gave way to the medieval city, merchants and artisans emerged as the nucleus of the new middle class, and the universities were founded in the cities. The mendicant orders of

St. Francis and St. Dominic arose to meet the religious challenges of this new age.

Other factors were woven into the fiber of the times. Crusaders had brought silks, satins, spices, and other luxuries of the East to the Western world. An attachment to luxurious living spread even among the clergy and monks. A fascination with courtly love was beginning in southern Europe; troubadours and love stories flourished. Paralleling this was the emergence of more sentimental devotions within the church. Hymns like "Jesu dulcis memoria" reflect the sweet flavor of this period. The humanity of Jesus and the Blessed Virgin were emphasized in the developing spirituality of the age, as were devotions to the passion of Christ, the blood of Christ, the five wounds, and many other devotions centered around the humanity of Christ.

Theological factors also contributed to the mendicant response. The friars were founded to combat a rising tide of heresy at the time. Ronald Knox speaks of the "underworld of the Middle Ages."[16] It was made up of two currents, the Catharist movement and the Waldensian movement, both of which contributed to the Albigensian heresy.

The Catharist heresy, very much like the Manichaean heresy, held that material things were evil—the body, the state, the visible church. Therefore bodily asceticism and fasting almost to the point of death were considered right and proper. Given the context of wealth and luxury from the Crusades, this movement made sense to many people and stimulated a great enthusiasm among them.

Side by side with this was the Waldensian movement, named after Peter Waldo of Lyons. In the famine year of 1176, he gave away his property and tried to live out the very letter of the Commandments and the poverty that he thought Christ proposed in the Gospels. The Waldensians were at first orthodox Christians, and the message that they proclaimed was quite legitimate, but they eventually became heretics who rejected the institutional church. The Waldensians developed into a sizeable movement, and their distinguishing marks were poverty, Bible reading, and itinerant preaching.

The Cathars, Waldensians, and others were reacting to specific evils in the church and in society. The Dominican prior of Louvain, Thomas of Chantimpre wrote, "I met on the street an abbot with so many horses and so large a retinue that if I had not known him I would have taken him for a duke or a count. Only the addition of a circlet on his brow would have been needed."[17]

It was in this sort of a world that the Dominicans were formally approved as an order in 1216, with the Franciscans gaining approval in 1223. The times urgently needed friars who could go out of their monasteries and combat the world's evils and errors. Humbert of Romans remarks in his commentary on Dominic's Rule, "Our order has been founded for preaching and for the salvation of our neighbors. Our studies should tend principally, ardently, above everything, to make us useful for souls."[18] St. Francis makes the same point when he records that he felt the most ecstatic joy when he heard the voice of God, "that it behooved him by preaching to convert many people. Thus says the Lord, 'Say to Brother Francis that God has not called him into this estate for himself alone, but to the end that he may gain fruit of souls and that many through him may be saved.'"[19]

This mission to others is the essential element in the mendicant transition. The Dominicans differed from the monastic tradition chiefly in that they had no vow of stability. The Dominicans did not live in isolation, and they maintained a careful, realistic poverty. They devoted themselves to Scripture study and to secular learning. The Dominican Rule allows a person to be excused from common prayer for the sake of study. This would be quite unthinkable in a strictly monastic tradition.

Even though the Franciscans and Dominicans were founded about the same time and were responding to similar challenges, the two orders have distinguishing characteristics. Dominic's Order was an order of priests from the start; Francis was never a priest. The founding of the Dominicans was altogether sober and unromantic, while much of the Italian romantic tradition is found in the Order of St. Francis. The Dominicans devoted themselves to both religious and secular study, while the earliest Franciscans were not generally interested in intellectual pursuits. The Dominicans turned their attention to the universities of Europe, while the Franciscans engaged themselves more in social and pastoral work.

The Dominicans were a community of priests who lived a monastic common life and performed direct apostolic service. Dominic placed great emphasis on organization with a high degree of monastic discipline. However, the discipline was modified to fit a vigorous apostolic life.

The Franciscans sprang from a voluntary poverty movement that existed at the time. It was also something of a youth movement that flourished in the cities. The movement was directed against the soft secularity of a Christianity that was making itself quite at home in the political and economic world around it.

Quite early in their history the Franciscans experienced an internal conflict over the interpretation of their poverty. A split developed between the Spirituals, who wanted to follow a very strict poverty, and the Observants, later known as the Order of Friars Minor, who wanted a more relaxed approach. In 1322 the pope condemned the Spirituals, but the split continued. From the Observant branch sprang several reform movements, the best known of which was the Capuchins.

The number of mendicant friars grew rapidly; by the early fourteenth century there were fifteen thousand Dominicans and thirty-five thousand Franciscans. Together with Augustinians and Carmelites, they constituted an army of more than eighty thousand mendicants at work throughout Christendom.

More important than the early history of these orders was a theological problem that underlaid the whole mendicant movement. The friars were intensely involved in apostolic activity, more so than any other religious group before them had been, but the traditions of monasticism were deeply inscribed in their religious attitudes. This ambiguity shows up clearly in the life and writing of Thomas à Kempis. His book *The Imitation of Christ,* a compilation from various sources, reflects the religious thinking of an entire age.

In one place à Kempis tells the reader, "Never be idle or vagrant. Be always reading or writing or praying or meditating, or employed in some useful labor for the common good."[20] This "common good" was no longer restricted to the monastic community, and à Kempis and his companions were engaged in teaching. Nevertheless, we also find this warning in the *Imitation of Christ:* "Fly from the tumult of men as much as you can. We seldom return to silence without prejudice to our conscience. As often as I have been among men, I have returned less a man. It is better to lie hidden and to take care of oneself than to neglect oneself even to work miracles."[21] This ambivalence between flight from the world and involvement in it is characteristic of the spirituality of the age and forms its most pressing problem—the need for an understanding of the spiritual life that does not merely allow for apostolic engagement but sees that very engagement as a source of holiness.

The ambiguity in à Kempis is also found in Thomas Aquinas. For St. Thomas, the contemplative life, absolutely considered, is better than the active, an attitude reflecting the influence of Pseudo-Dionysius and the Origenist spirituality. But Thomas also says that the "mixed" life is the highest form of life. "Just as it is better to illuminate than merely to shine, so to pass on what one has contemplated *(contemplata aliis tradere)* is better than merely to contemplate."[22] But we notice here that the active life is appraised from its contemplative element (which is higher) and not from the intrinsic worth of the apostolic work itself. So the problem remains and is heightened through this period of the mendicant transition. Can active apostolic work by itself promote union with God? Can it be justified on its own intrinsic worth? When the monk leaves his prie-dieu is he necessarily farther from God? Is there no theory that will esteem and justify the active life on its own merits alone? Until the sixteenth century no satisfactory answer to these questions would appear.

The Religious Climate of the Later Middle Ages

The fourteenth and fifteenth centuries were a time of momentous transition and turmoil in western Europe. This was the time of the Black Death, the Hundred Years' War, and the Great Western Schism where at one point three rival popes vied to rule Christendom. This was also the era of piety represented in *The Imitation of Christ.* Our picture of the spirituality of the great religious families of Dominic and Francis must be balanced by a more general picture of the religious climate of the times. In his book *The Waning of the Middle Ages,* Johan Huizinga writes:

> To the world when it was half a thousand years younger the outline of all things seemed more clearly marked than they do to us. Life seemed to consist in extremes—a fierce religious asceticism and an unrestrained licentiousness, ferocious judicial punishments and great popular waves of pity and mercy, the most horrible crimes and the most extravagant acts of saintliness—and everywhere a sea of tears. All experience had yet to the minds of men the directness and absoluteness of the pleasure and pain of child life. Every event, every action, was still embodied in

> expressive and solemn forms which raised them to the dignity of ritual. For it was not merely the great facts of birth, marriage and death which, by the sacredness of the sacraments, were raised to the rank of mysteries; incidents of less importance, like a journey, a task, a visit, were equally attended by a thousand formalities: benedictions, ceremonies, formulae.[23]

Europeans in the later Middle Ages held two different attitudes toward the life of prayer and communion with God. One attitude developed from the Benedictine tradition and proposed a process of natural development through liturgy and *lectio divina.* This type of prayer is marked by spontaneity, simplicity, and naturalness following the direction of the Holy Spirit. The other attitude stressed a cult of contemplation, a methodical series of psychological techniques for achieving a state of unknowing—a union with God in a very abstruse sense.

This second type of prayer flourished among the Rhineland mystics in the fourteenth century. The best known were the great mystic and teacher Meister Eckhart and his three disciples, Johann Tauler, Blessed Henry Suso, and Blessed Jan van Ruysbroeck. This was the second great period of mysticism in the church (the first being the third- and fourth-century Eastern monastic period). Once again, people wrote and talked freely about their mystical experiences.

These Rhineland mystics were basically in the Pseudo-Dionysian tradition and used his vocabulary. The goal was the abandonment of material things for union with God. Eckhart says, for example, "One should pray with such energy that he would wish all his limbs, and all his strength, his eyes, ears, mouth, heart, and all his senses were straining within him. He should not cease until he seems to have become one with Him who is present and to whom he prays."[24] Eckhart was condemned for "pantheism" because it seemed in his effort to articulate his experience that the self merged into God and was lost.

When trying to understand these mystics, we must realize that it is very difficult for people to express mystical experiences in writing. They were struggling for some way to express what was a genuine gift of God, and human language is quite inadequate to the task. Misunderstanding due to the limitations of language is almost inevitable.

Eckhart explains that when one has achieved a state of union with God, he is in "the abyss without mode and without form of the silent and waste divinity."[25] The fruition of bliss says Van Ruysbroeck, "is so immense that God himself is as swallowed up with all the blessed in an absence of modes, which is a not-knowing, and in an eternal loss of self."[26] This idea of knowledge of God that is above all knowing is characteristic of this school of mysticism. Eckhart teaches that in the final stage of mystical union the soul is "buried in the Godhead" and "is God Himself"[27] enjoying all things, disposing all things as God himself does.

Another group of mystics who continued the Dionysian and Rhineland tradition appeared in England. Richard Rolle, a sort of freelance hermit, wrote a great deal about the advantages of the contemplative and mystical life (although it seems that he was not a mystic himself). Walter Hilton wrote *The Scale of Perfection,* and another mystic, whose name is unknown, wrote two books, *The Cloud of Unknowing* and *The Epistle of Privy Counsel.*

One English mystic who should be singled out is Dame Julian of Norwich. Her one work, *The Revelations of Divine Love,* is a book of such theological depth and poetic beauty that it is perhaps the greatest single piece of devotional writing in the English language. Dame Julian's mysticism reaches out to others. She stresses the great wonders of God, a God who acts in history and controls history and who will make all things well in the end. Her basic theme is confidence in the divine love as the ultimate reality behind the universe and in the midst of the history of the world.

However, neither Benedictine spirituality nor mysticism captures the spirit of the religious imagination of the time. Popular religion was characterized by an all-prevailing attempt to raise all the details of daily life to the level of the sacred and to find religious meaning in the most commonplace activity. Every object and action, however trivial, was constantly correlated with Christ and salvation. Blessed Henry Suso, for example, would eat three-quarters of an apple in the name of the Trinity, and the remaining quarter in commemoration of the love with which the heavenly Mother gave her tender child Jesus an apple to eat. For this reason he ate the last quarter with the paring, since little boys do not peel their apples. After Christmas he did not eat it, for then the infant Jesus was too young to eat apples.[28]

This sounds humorous, but this attempt to superimpose religious significance on all the events in which one is engaged is one solution to the problem of how to justify action that is not contemplation. It is a practical, not a theoretical, solution. However, this effort is psychologically impossible to sustain. It leads neither to a genuine prayer life nor to effective performance of day-to-day activities.

Perceptive church leaders at this time warned that spirituality was being overloaded. A position paper prepared for the Council of Constance in 1414 pointed this out. It argued that this type of spirituality so flooded the mind with religious images that normal and balanced life was upset. There was too much quantity without quality.

Another problem was that the legitimately sacred things that should be given reverence were lost in the confusion. The veneration of relics, for example, became mixed with crude primitive ideas and superstitions. The monks at Fossanuova, for instance, for fear of losing the body of Thomas Aquinas, decapitated it, boiled it, and preserved it.

Saints and saint legends multiplied in this period. There was a saint for every conceivable occupation, every town, every house, and for preservation from every possible disease and calamity.

People lost track of what constituted sanctity. If it had been up to the people at large, Blessed Peter of Luxembourg would have been canonized by popular acclaim. He was made bishop of Metz at the age of fifteen and became a cardinal a year later. He carried out a total chastisement of his body denying himself food and every possible convenience. During the last years of his life he always kept his confessor at his side and used to wake up at night in order to go to confession. At his death numerous little slips of paper were found on which Peter had noted down his various faults; he used these in preparation for confession and for meditation on his own unworthiness and sinfulness. He died at the age of eighteen. The cause for his canonization was immediately introduced by no fewer than three kings and the faculty of the University of Paris.

Why did the religious imagination of this period tend to develop such extremes? Perhaps because there was insufficient nourishment for a healthy spirituality. Despite the corrective legislation of councils and synods, preaching in general remained relatively poor. Vernacular translations of the Bible were often suspect, if not forbidden; and the Mass itself became increasingly distant and unintelligible. The mystics may also have contributed to the problem. Some of the visionaries fed popular imagination and practice with extravagances that were at best peripheral to a healthy spirituality.

The people of the later Middle Ages were not morally worse or less religious than those of other ages. The evidence actually indicates the opposite—they had an enormous amount of religious energy, but it was an energy too often unbridled. When the Protestant Reformation split the church, its program was, in significant measure, an attack on the kind of distortions I have been describing.

The Catholic answer to all this was the great Council of Trent. Yet it is legitimate to ask whether this council was more concerned in some areas with symptoms than with underlying causes. At the level of doctrinal theology, it produced some remarkable decrees, and it succeeded in inaugurating a comprehensive system of moral and doctrinal training for the clergy. But the council fathers did not heed many legitimate concerns about the spiritual life.

The Nature of Mysticism

Anyone interested in the dynamics of spirituality must know something about the nature of mysticism and the theology of it. I will try to present here an outline of the traditional teaching of the theologians on mysticism. Mysticism is not a private phenomenon; it happens in the church and adds to the richness of the church's life.

Two crucial elements must be presupposed in any genuine mystical life. One is a certain amount of genuine moral striving toward perfection on the part of the individual. People at odds with God do not become mystics. Many mystics, of course, were not saints, but anybody involved in genuine mysticism displays a moral orientation toward perfection. Secondly, mysticism is a wholly gratuitous gift of God, which he gives to whom he pleases.

Mysticism can be defined as the direct and experiential awareness of God's presence in the depths of one's person. This direct awareness of God is unmediated knowledge. In all ordinary human knowledge, words, images, concepts, and symbols have a necessary and essential function. Not so in mystical experience. Mystical knowledge bypasses these; it is unmediated.

Mystical knowledge also differs from the ordinary knowledge of faith. By faith, people know that God is present within them, but they are not aware of this experientially. The mystic is somehow actually grasped by God. Some mystics struggle to express this as "tastes" of God and "touches" of God. Mystics try to indicate something that cannot be described in words and concepts, and so they resort to sense expressions of taste and touch to describe the experience of God. Finally, mysticism touches the very depths of a person's being. All defenses and facades are totally bypassed. God touches a person at the most basic level.

Despite these common denominators we have just pointed out, there is a great diversity in mystics and mysticism, the diversity of many different temperaments reacting to the one great reality that is God. The experience of mysticism itself must be carefully distinguished from its possible concomitants: ecstasy, visions, stigmata, levitations, and so on.

Mystical visions are traditionally classified into three types: corporeal, imaginative, and intellectual. A corporeal vision is an experience in which a person sees or hears something that is actually physically present outside his imagination. An imaginative vision will seem entirely the same as the corporeal, but it is actually entirely within the imagination. This does not make the imaginative vision any less genuine. An intellectual vision is an experience of insight or realization with no perceptible sense elements.

Are there corporeal visions? Many have doubts whether there have ever been such visions. John of the Cross and Teresa of Ávila, among others, hold that mystical visions are imaginative rather than corporeal. The question of placing these visions within the context of mysticism still remains. The traditional understanding is that visions are not directly caused by God, but are rather an overflow of a more central, purely spiritual process, that of infused contemplation. Thus, it depends somewhat on a person's temperament whether or not, or how, the intimate contact with God overflows into a vision.

That the form of visions depends on the mystic's temperament also explains the historical and psychological content of visions and shows how errors can occur in them. In other words, what God directly causes in visions is the intimate mystical union with himself. He does not directly cause the concomitant experience, which may manifest itself in a vision. That experience will be determined partially by the mystical experience of God and partially by the person's own experience and mental makeup.

The case of St. Margaret Mary Alacoque illustrates the historical and psychological determinations in visions. St. Margaret had visions of the Sacred Heart of Jesus, which included imagery of a flame, a crown of thorns, and a cross above the heart. Where did they come from? St. Margaret was a Visitation nun, and all of these symbols were present in the pictorial and devotional traditions of the Visitation Order for some time. The mystical experience did not infuse new images and pictures into her mind. The images were already there; they simply became more clearly focused and more effectively organized as a result of the mystical experience.

The ultimate test for determining the authenticity of a mystical experience has always been an increase in a person's virtue. By their fruits you shall know them. If God truly establishes a unique union in the depths of a soul, it can only result in a much greater degree of humility and charity in the life of the person. This is the only sure criterion. The great mystics of the church have always been suspicious of visions and the other concomitant phenomena. History confirms the opinion of a leading theologian that three out of four "visions," even of pious and "normal" people, are pure hallucinations.

Finally there is the question of personal or ecclesial mysticism. Personal visions are those whose object and content solely concern the perfection of the individual who has them. Ecclesial or prophetic visions are those that induce or commission the visionary to issue a message or warning requiring something, or even on occasion those that foretell the future.[29]

The revelations to St. Margaret Mary Alacoque also illustrate the ecclesial function of mysticism. The church in the seventeenth century was deeply influenced by Jansenism, a movement that stressed an austere piety and a rigorously puritanical morality. The good news of God's redemptive love for humankind was being widely ignored. St. Margaret Mary Alacoque's private revelations of the Sacred Heart called the church to pay attention to the fundamental reality of Christ's unfailing love for human beings. Thus, the mystical graces granted to St. Margaret Mary were eventually for the good and benefit of the whole church.

Though our own age and culture are generally unsympathetic to mysticism, it is too much a part of the history of the church to be cast aside. We should respect genuine mysticism.

But where does one find genuine mysticism? The attitude of the church has always been one of extreme caution in this regard. Perhaps this should be our attitude as well—caution and respect, along with appreciation of the immense good that has come to the church from the authentic mystics.

Ignatian Prayer: Finding God in All Things

The common ground of all spiritualities is an effort to achieve union with God, but the history of spirituality reveals many different ideas about who God is, what he is doing, and how he might be approached. In the Eastern spirituality of Evagrius, Pseudo-Dionysius, and Cassian, the idea of God showed strong Neoplatonic influences: God the supreme transcendent Mind, the pure, immutable One. The approach to this God was an effort toward a union of minds, the human with the divine. Contemplation became the ideal of Christian life and perfection. This doctrine has influenced religious thinking down to our own day.

A simpler, more human, less angelic method of prayer was proposed by St. Benedict: the chanting of the Divine Office and the quiet, meditative reading of the sacred Scripture. Both of these forms of prayer require recollection and some withdrawal from other forms of activity. At least implicit in this approach is that God is thought of chiefly in his transcendence. The Benedictine-influenced ideal of spirituality still centers around the periods of formal prayer carried on away from the world in the quiet of the oratory or cell.

The apostolic demand that Gregory I made upon the Benedictines set the conditions for the prayer-action problem that has existed for centuries in the history of spirituality. The problem is simply stated: how do we justify activity and work in the world when the ideal of Christian perfection is union with God achieved through some type of formal prayer? The difficulty remained up until the sixteenth century, when, for the first time, someone proposed that union with God could be sought and found in the world among men. The man who proposed this was St. Ignatius Loyola.

The revolution in spiritual thinking and practice brought about by St. Ignatius centered around a different idea of God, where he was, what he was doing, and how he might be found. And this led to a radically new kind of prayer and spirituality. With a great mystical grace, Ignatius received a vision of God and the world that could resolve the prayer-action dilemma.

The God of Ignatius is he who works *magnalia Dei*—the mighty acts of God in the world. We see a new, more biblical emphasis on God's immanent activity in the world. God continually works the creation of the world, and, in the person of Jesus Christ, he works the redemption of mankind. The God of Ignatius is not deistic or remote. He dwells in creatures and "works and labors for me in all of them."[30]

This notion of God gives rise to a different spirituality. Earlier writers conceived of the spiritual life as a union with God in interior prayer; Ignatius, struck by God's action in the world, was convinced that a person could achieve a union with

God in action as well as in contemplation. The operative principle is a union of human will with God's will. Ignatius believed that to find God's will is to find God, and to do God's will, even in total activity, is to be totally united with God. The person imbued with Ignatian spirituality is one who works with God the worker.

For Ignatius, this union with God in action is prayer. In essence, Ignatius expands the notion of prayer to include activity. The basic principle of Ignatian spirituality is to "find God in all things." The object is a union with God that, for Ignatius, can be achieved in prayer in the traditional sense, in action by a union of will with God, and in an awareness of God's presence in the world.

Ignatius insisted on the necessity of formal prayer. The *Spiritual Exercises,* his famous guide to the spiritual life, is a collection of meditations, contemplations, and vocal prayers that Ignatius required all of his followers to make. The time of formal prayer could be used for the discernment of spirits, for finding God's will, for fostering one's sense of the grandeur of God's action in the world, or for simple conversation with God. Yet Ignatius discouraged prolonged prayer of this type as a daily practice. For him, this type of prayer was a means in, and not the end of, the spiritual life. This view was Ignatius's radical departure from the contemplative ideal of other spiritualities.

A second aspect of "finding God in all things" is the Ignatian emphasis on direct action based upon a union of will. "Casting off the last vestiges of the Neoplatonic techniques, Ignatius affirms that the Christian mystical union is essentially the union of love where correspondence to the divine will is more important than psychological techniques and which can therefore be acquired no matter what the circumstances."[31]

According to this kind of prayer, it is sufficient to seek to discover God's will and then to carry it out vigorously with full attention on the work to be done with no concomitant vision or contemplation. "In activity and in study, . . . when we direct everything to the service of God, everything is prayer."[32] Ignatius had an enriched and broader notion of prayer than previous spiritual leaders. For him "the word 'prayer' means now a disinterested prayer which is established in the solitude of the heart and then the spiritual attitude which causes us to 'find God' in the midst of activity, even the most absorbing. On the one hand, prayer is considered as a particular and definite 'exercise' and, on the other, the continuous union with God in activity."[33]

Because a union of will in action is his primary approach to union with God, Ignatius puts great emphasis on obedience and a right intention in all things. He also stresses the importance of discernment of spirits because discernment is of crucial value in discovering the will of God. Ignatian union of will with God must not be thought of as mechanical or military. For Ignatius the motive force and the essence of this union was always a personal love of God.

While reserving a place for formal prayer, Ignatius always preferred the prayer of action—collaboration with God in the great deeds that he does in the world. This makes for an action-oriented spirituality of total service for the kingdom of Christ. It is a spirituality that provides a theoretical support for apostolic work, and it explains how one who engages himself fully in the work is no farther from God than the contemplative in his quiet room. He may be closer.

In his writings, St. Ignatius uses the formula "finding God in all things" in still another sense to describe a certain perceptual awareness of the presence of God in the world. This is something he experienced daily and that in some analogous form he recommended to his followers. Jerome Nadal wrote of Ignatius that "in all things, actions, conversations, he felt and contemplated the presence of God and the attraction of spiritual things. He was a contemplative in action, something he expressed habitually in the words: we must find God in all things."[34] This peculiar prayer was the result of mystical graces of a very high order. Indeed, Ignatius is ranked with the greatest mystics in the history of the church.

Despite the gratuity of Ignatius's own gifts, we find that he used the same formula, 'to find God in all things,' to recommend a form of prayer to young Jesuits in training. These men, who certainly were not expected to have had the mystical graces that he had, were advised to seek God in all things:

> Considering the end of study, the scholastics can hardly give themselves to prolonged meditation. Over and above the spiritual exercises assigned for their perfection, namely daily Mass, an hour for vocal prayer and examen of conscience, weekly confession and communion, they should exercise themselves in seeking our Lord's presence in all things, in their conversation, their walks, in what they see, taste, hear, understand, and in everything they do, since it is clear that His divine majesty is in all things by his presence, power, and essence. And this kind of meditation which finds God our Lord in all things is

> easier than raising oneself to the consideration of divine truths which are more abstract and demand more of an effort if we are to keep our attention on them.[35]

Ignatius here recommends a simpler kind of prayer than the formulas of contemplation, a prayer that focuses upon the omnipresence of God with special emphasis upon his immanence in things, persons, situations, and experiences. Ignatius's "contemplation in action" is purged of all Neoplatonic overtones that suggest an interior exercise carried on in solitude and silence. It is rather a wide-awake, eyes-open sort of thing that seeks to find God who is present and active in the world, in history, in the activities of men. In the midst of activity, the apostle may sense that what he is doing is God's work, that God is present and active in him and in the situation. It is an ongoing sense or awareness that God is active here. Jean Danielou, a twentieth-century Jesuit theologian, says that the Ignatian man

> ought to be a saint and he ought to live in complete activity. Previous spirituality opposed these two aspects. Activity seemed to be an obstacle to holiness which was conceived as contemplation. The revolution accomplished by St. Ignatius showed that that which appeared to be an obstacle could become a means. To the heart filled with God, all things speak of Him. And it is not a question merely of an orientation of the will, but of a spiritual experience where God is "tasted" in everything.[36]

The language of sense experience keeps recurring in the description of this kind of prayer, and along with it the indication that there are many different degrees of this finding God in all things. At one end there is the basic union of will with the simple conviction and satisfaction that "I am doing what God wants me to do." At the other pole is great mystical experience, a constant awareness of the presence of God in all things, the highest perfection of the virtue of faith. Says Danielou:

> It would be imprudent to believe that one could go very quickly to God through creatures. . . . St. Francis of Assisi chanted the Canticle of the Sun, but only after having been the stigmatist of Alverno. What St. Ignatius describes to us then is an idea of consummated perfection, of a soul so totally filled with God that everything leads to God. Thus, the spiritual itinerary takes place completely between the moment when creatures are obstacles and the moment they become means. . . . According to the words of St. Ignatius, "He loves God in all creatures and all creatures in God."[37]

The Contemplative Climate in Sixteenth-Century Spain

In every age of the church, God reveals himself in the sacred Scriptures, but not every age sees the message clearly and in proper perspective. To correct this vision can be one of the functions of the ecclesial mystic. Under God's direction, the mystic discerns something in the Scripture that a whole age may have failed to perceive. Ignatius Loyola seems to have performed this function in sixteenth-century Spain. The religious climate with its contemplative ideal was quite contrary to that of Ignatius Loyola. To understand Ignatius's place in the history of spirituality, it is helpful to understand something of the religious and cultural background of his times.

Spain was the great power of the sixteenth century. The Spanish people had just successfully concluded an eight-hundred-year struggle to drive the Moors out of Spain, and they were basking in the glory of their triumph. Spain had the finest army and navy in the world. Much of Europe—the Austrian Empire, the Low Countries, and much of Italy—was under Spanish control. But Spaniards were proudest of the fact that the people were all Catholic. Spain was untainted by the Protestant Reformation, and this was her greatest glory.

Sixteenth-century Spain witnessed a full flowering of the baroque spirit, which was epitomized in the Escorial, the royal palace of Philip II. This huge complex of palace, fortress, library, and church was built around 1560 as a monument to the Catholic victory over the Moors. The Escorial, a contemporary historian has written, is a confession of Catholicity born of the Spanish soul. Here we see the king's longing for unity; he did not want to rule over heretics. The architecture aims at the expression of spiritual things; God is the intended goal. In the church, the eucharistic liturgy and the Divine Office are celebrated eight hours a day. The adoration of the Blessed Sacrament was continuous, with no fewer than one hundred monks constantly employed in this task. The complex included a great library, for God must be served here, too, in study and scholarship. But in the midst of all this splendor and greatness we find the king himself living as a simple monk in an austere apartment, the most humble of the servants of the Lord.[38] We see here greatness of soul together with religious devotion, penance, and renunciation.

The contemplative ideal of this age was strongly mystical. A historian of the period claims that there were no fewer than three thousand writers on the contemplative life and mysticism in sixteenth-century Spain. The mystical ideal had captivated the religious imagination of the age. If one wished to be a perfect Christian, one would have to go to a monastery and become a contemplative monk or nun.

This identification of the contemplative life and Christian perfection gained great impetus from the writings of two great mystics of the period, John of the Cross and Teresa of Ávila. They wrote about their own deep mystical experiences and profoundly influenced the popular religious imagination. Many Spaniards sought the same kind of experience of the intimate touch of God in mystical union. This was the perfection of the Christian life.

Along with the glories of sixteenth-century Spanish mysticism came dangers, delusions, and excesses, particularly in a kind of latent heresy called illuminism. Those identified with the movement, known as the *Alumbrados* or Illuminati, claimed to have reached such a height of mystical union with God that it was no longer necessary for them to pay any attention to any authority, even the hierarchical church. They thought that if one had direct contact with God in mystical experience, it was no longer possible to commit sin or to be mistaken in one's religious ideas.

The Inquisition, which was also at the height of its power in Spain at this time, went after the Alumbrados. Many of them were questioned and imprisoned. The Inquisition sucessfully stamped out much of this Alumbrado movement.

This spiritual climate exercised a profound influence on the Society of Jesus. At the death of Ignatius Loyola in 1556, more than half, perhaps almost two-thirds, of all Jesuits came from this Spain that I have been describing—the Spain that had such a tremendous longing for mystical union with God, for flight from the world, for identifying Christian perfection with the contemplative life. Thus it is no surprise that the Society was deeply affected by these religious currents after the death of Ignatius.

Ignatian Prayer, Second Generation

Within the context of sixteenth-century piety, we have noted that Ignatian spirituality is characterized by an interior disposition of soul by which one's union with God is centered about wholehearted action for the greater glory of God and the kingdom of Christ. The interior aspect of union of wills is exteriorly manifested by tireless, loving service of the church, whatever her immediate needs may be. In Ignatius's vision it is precisely this ceaseless and unselfish labor that detaches the apostle from himself and centers him more and more on Christ, and so the work becomes an exercise of prayer and union with God.

This orientation toward apostolic labor produces a challenge of its own—the possible neglect of formal prayer. Ignatius held that both prayer and action done according to God's will are basically two aspects of the same thing, the love of God. But while this was clear to Ignatius himself, one might ask how he expressed this in the Constitutions of the Society and how the fathers who followed him interpreted and altered this Constitution.

In the Constitutions of the Society of Jesus, Ignatius prescribed that every applicant to the order make the thirty-day Spiritual Exercises. This was expected to culminate in a personal conversion and commitment. The young Jesuit was educated in a school of prayer and became a "mortified" man, not one who fasted twenty-four hours but one who was oriented toward God and saw him above everything else. Ignatius did not expect the mental prayer of the Exercises to be a permanent form of prayer for all his followers. For Ignatius, prayer was a style of life—something organic that grows under its own power and the guidance of the Holy Spirit and that issues in a life of prayerful action.

The Constitutions of the Society, approved in 1558, did outline a certain varied and flexible program of spiritual practices, but no single program was obligatory for all Jesuits. For young men in training, the program called for weekly communion and confession, daily Mass, and one hour of prayer that was to include the two examens, the office of the Blessed Virgin, and other prayers of their liking. All this was to be under the oversight of a spiritual director.

For Jesuits who had been admitted to final vows in the Society, Ignatius wrote that

> it must be taken for certain that they will be spiritual men . . . so progressed in the way of Christ our Lord that they can run in it as much as their care for health and external works of charity and obedience will allow. . . . For chastisement of the body it does not seem necessary that any regulation be written down except that mature charity will dictate whatever is necessary for each one.

> Nevertheless, let each one's confessor always be consulted and whenever any question comes up about what should be done, let the matter be brought to the superior.[39]

Mature charity under direction is Ignatius's universal principle for designing the spiritual life. These were essential elements of the Constitution and Ignatius would never consider changing any one of them. He said explicitly that it was "his opinion from which no one would ever move him that for those who are studying, one hour of prayer was sufficient, it being supposed they are practicing mortification and self denial."[40] When Ignatius's deputy Jerome Nadal visited the Spanish provinces and yielded to their request for one-and-a-half hours of daily prayer, Ignatius was angered. According to Nadal, "Thereafter he did not make great use of my services."[41]

Ignatius stood for freedom and flexibility in the individual's spiritual life. One's prayer life was to be determined under the guidance of the Holy Spirit and the spiritual director, and prayer must be shaped to meet the individual's personal needs and abilities. Now this sort of attitude is not peculiar to Ignatius; it is true of many great founders of religious communities. But pressures soon arise as institutions expand, which tends to encourage the programming of performance in order to secure and ensure certain ideals of the organization. This is just what happened with Jesuit prayer in the second generation.

Internal pressures to standardize prayer soon arose within the Jesuits after Ignatius's death. Spanish and Portuguese superiors feared that a tepidity was creeping into the Society in matters of humility and obedience, and they wanted regulations set up regarding prayer. To bolster the humility and obedience, especially in the younger men, these superiors attempted to prescribe a certain amount of time for formal prayer. This was consistent, of course, with the contemplative context in which they were living. Reform movements also have a way of programming things in order to ensure their objectives. For example, Francis Borgia, the third general of the Society of Jesus, had lived in a Spanish community where the priests and scholastics were accustomed to spending three hours a day in prayer and meditation. When Borgia became general of the Society, he prescribed one hour of meditation a day. The wonder is why he did not order more.

The rapid numerical increase of members in the Society was another factor that tended to dilute the original fervor and spirit and seemed to call for some sort of remedial action. The non-Jesuit contemplative tradition, especially in Spain, created another pressure for an increased amount of obligatory prayer for all. Ignatius withstood this environmental pressure; his followers apparently could not.

Pressures for a prescribed amount of obligatory prayer divided the early Jesuits. Jesuits in northern Europe, France, Holland, and Germany resisted any change in the Constitutions, while those in southern Europe—the majority, chiefly from Spain and Italy—argued for a change.

The Second General Congregation in 1565 elected Francis Borgia superior general and left the matter of increased prescribed prayer up to him to decide. One month after he was elected, Borgia prescribed the full hour of prayer for all members of the Society.

Other prayers were added. In 1566 Pope Pius V asked the Society to say regular litanies for the resolution of the Turkish problem in eastern Europe. This temporary request became prescribed and institutionalized; Jesuits said the litanies regularly until recent years. Rosaries came to be worn with cassocks because Father Borgia wore one. In 1572 prescribed spiritual reading was introduced.

By the time of the Third Congregation (1573), a considerable movement had developed within the Society to return to the original spirit and letter of the Constitutions of St. Ignatius in the matter of prayer. A number of provincial superiors made the request, but Father General Mecurian simply refused to yield on the practice of Father Borgia. *"Nihil innovandum est."* No innovation was to be made on Borgia's innovation! But dispensations were allowed for the weak and for foreseeable conflicts.

The practice of obligatory prayer introduced a new problem that appears most pointedly in a letter written to the general in 1576 by the French provincial, Father Claude Matheieu.

> Will your paternity please consider whether in the Society it is fitting that the period of time for prayer be observed which is prescribed in the Constitutions, and that the increase of prayer be removed which was introduced some years ago. For I notice that Ours are less fervent in prayer now than previously. Indeed in the past they often used to ask permission to give more time to prayer, and perhaps they spent more time then on prayer than they do now. . . . But nowadays many ask to be dispensed from the increase in prayer. Thus in a very short time there will be more people who are dispensed, or what is worse, more people who will dispense themselves, than those who, as

> is now the case, observe the rule. It has always seemed to me that we will accomplish not a little if we simply and perfectly observe those things which are in our Constitutions, because if we wish to adopt other things, there is fear that little by little the practice of what is prescribed in our Constitutions will cease, and finally we will learn to our discomfort that it would have been better if we had remained in the simplicity of our fathers.[42]

Nevertheless, a legislated amount of daily prayer for Jesuits was solidly confirmed and entrenched at the end of the sixteenth century.

How can we interpret this development? It seems to be a normal and legitimate instance of institutionalization, a result of the effort to organize and stabilize a religious way of life. There can be no real objection to this. But a definite difficulty arises when one particular form of the development becomes "consecrated," institutionalized, and irreversible for subsequent generations. Times and cultures change, and what may have been a suitable embodiment of the Ignatian ideal in Francis Borgia's time (though this is open to question too), may not be at all suitable in another culture centuries later, and may not be suitable in our own time.

The development from Ignatius to his successors is something like the development from apostolic Christianity of the first century to the established Catholicism of the fourth and fifth. What happened was a routinization of religious life. The greatest danger here is not the change, but that a particular form of change should become inflexible and irreversible. Some regularization of religious spirit will be inevitable in a large religious community, but it should be constantly adaptable and adapted to various times and circumstances.

And then perhaps Ignatius's original working principle concerning prayer would still be the best of all: prayer as a style of life, a seeking to find God in all things, with formal prayer as a means of disposing the individual to do God's will, the time to be determined by mature charity under the guidance of the Holy Spirit and the spiritual father.

On the evidence presented, we can speak of a real distinction between Ignatian prayer and Jesuit prayer. But as we read the history of the past and question the legislation of another age, we must still discern and determine how best to adapt the spirit and ideal of a founder to the circumstances of our own time.

Finding God's Will: Discernment

In his book *The Love of God,* Dom Aelred Graham talks about the distinctive virtues of some of the great saints in the history of the church. The virtue most revealed in the life of St. Benedict, he says, was religion. In the life of St. Thomas Aquinas, faith joined with wisdom. In St. Ignatius, he suggests, the virtue is supernatural prudence and discernment. This virtue of Ignatius is one of the most misunderstood elements of his spirituality.

Ignatius Loyola learned the art of discernment through his efforts to interpret the profound spiritual experiences he had at the time of his conversion. We find the principles of this discernment described in the *Spiritual Exercises.* Ignatius considered the art of discernment the indispensable element of the Exercises. In a certain sense the whole purpose of a retreat is to learn how to discover the will of God, most especially how to choose among various alternative good possibilities of action.

But where is God's will? Which means will be most conducive to the honor and glory and the service and love of God? It is precisely at this point that Ignatius's Rules for the Discernment of Spirits apply. These rules are essential to Ignatian spirituality, but they also transcend it and are universally applicable in any Christian tradition.

At the outset it is important to note that for Ignatius there is no question whatsoever of choices for God's glory coming as a result of human initiative or ascetic discipline. Any human effort in this direction is initiated by the grace of Christ through the action of the Holy Spirit. So, also, the enemy of the church and of human nature, Satan, is spiritual and personal. Good and evil spirits are locked in a spiritual conflict, of which the primary battleground is the human heart. From patristic and medieval tradition, Ignatius took the idea that God, angels, and demons more or less regularly invade human consciousness, producing virtuous or sinful inclinations. Discernment is needed to identify the source of these impulses. We may not look on spirits precisely as Ignatius did, but the underlying reality is valid enough: powers of good and evil experienced as a kind of personal and powerful force taking hold of people.[43]

There are two different levels of discernment, and St. Ignatius divides them into two sets of rules. The first set goes with the First Week of the Spiritual Exercises, and the second set with the following weeks. The distinctive purpose of the First Week is to prepare individuals to receive the grace of God by examining some fundamental considerations about themselves and the world around them. One does this by locating oneself in the world in relationship to God, determining where one stands in this relationship, then assessing one's value system. Once this is done and the need for contact with God is realized, a person can then confront the distinctly Christian vocation of following Christ. Once individuals realize that God is an operative force in their life, they start to ask themselves how they can serve God better.

The first set of rules for discernment involves choosing between good and evil (First Week); the second set involves choosing among various alternative goods in order to follow Christ more closely (Second Week). When the choice is no longer between good and evil but among various goods, choices can become difficult, and individuals wonder how they can know whether a particular way of behaving or a particular choice is God's will. This is where discernment comes in.

Ignatius says that consolation and desolation are the two basic states of soul—the matter for discernment. Consolation is the complete love of God with an increase of faith, hope, charity, and interior joy. Desolation is the opposite: darkness of soul, turmoil of spirit, restlessness, temptations against faith, hope, and love.

For a person going from one mortal sin to another, the evil spirit presents apparent pleasures, sensual delights, and gratifications. To the same person, the good spirit causes remorse and the sting of conscience.

For one moving from sin to love of God, the spirits act the very opposite: the evil one harasses with anxiety, sadness, and obstacles; the good spirit gives courage, strength, consolation, and peace.

To begin discernment, people must know the basic orientation of their lives and develop a keen sensitivity about how they feel. When we are experiencing desolation, Ignatius advises that we be patient, realize that God has left us on our own, and be assured that God will give sufficient grace to overcome that state of soul. When we experience consolation, we should store up strength against desolation and humbly recognize the source of our well-being.

Ignatius then exposes three tactical maneuvers of the enemy: (1) He is weak in the face of strong resistance to temptation, and a tyrant if he has the upper hand; (2) he also acts like a false lover who seeks to remain hidden and wants his proposals and actions kept secret; if his seductions and temptations are revealed to a confessor or another person, he knows he cannot succeed; and (3) the enemy is like a military commander who attacks a stronghold at its weakest point, so he will assault individuals with temptations where their virtue is weakest.

These Rules for the First Week are fairly straightforward. One is just becoming sensitive to experiences in the spiritual life; the basic choice is between sin and nonsin, and the lines are fairly clearly drawn between good and evil. But as people advance in the spiritual life, their decisions become somewhat more subtle because they are making choices among alternative goods.

In the Rules for the Second Week, the presuppositions are rather different. They suppose that there are definite movements, feelings, and impulses going on in the soul, and that the person is sensitive to them. The choice is now among alternative good courses of action, this or that way of life, this or that mission where the choice is open and all the possibilities are good. Then the distinctions between the various choices are not too clear, but complex and sometimes confused.

An example from Jean-Paul Sartre's book *Existentialism and Humanism* illustrates the situation of a person trying to discover the greater good. A pupil of Sartre's during the Nazi occupation of France was anxious to decide whether he ought to leave home and join the Free French forces or stay at home and help his mother, who was sick and very much dependent on him. These were two good alternatives, and the young man was torn between the demands of filial devotion and patriotic generosity. No one could settle the problem for him; in the last analysis the student himself would be responsible for his own choice. In advising him, Sartre goes on to say, "I had but one reply to make; You are free, therefore choose. That is to say, invent. No rule of general morality can show you what you ought to do. No signs are given in this world. We ourselves decide our being. . . . Decide your future, you alone are responsible for it."[44]

Here is a situation in which the general rules of morality do not provide a solution for a particular problem. The problem is not that it is difficult to decide what is right; rather, the issue is that it is simply impossible by Christian reason alone to know God's will precisely here and now. Ignatius proposes a solution. It is the method he describes in the Second Time of Choosing a State of Life, "when much light and understanding are derived through experience of desolations and consolations and discernment of diverse spirits."[45]

Ignatius insists that we focus our attention not on the choices but on the involuntary movements of the heart. We feel consolation or not, desolation or not, and there is nothing we can do about it. Ignatius urges that we pay close attention to these feelings because it is in them that the good and evil spirits are at work, and through them that we can discern the will of God.

The consolation that is strongly indicative is that which comes to the soul "without any previous cause."[46] This is given by God alone. No perceivable cause or object produces it; it is self-validating. This consolation is felt as a conscious experience of grace, of the love of God, in which the soul is drawn "wholly to the love of His Divine Majesty."[47]

Ignatius says this consolation may occur in the context of a choice of a way of life, so that as a person considers one alternative, he or she may experience peace, joy, tranquility, enthusiasm, or simply openness to God. The right decision leaves the consolation of the union with God intact. This is the spirit of God confirming a person in this particular choice. There is a certain congruousness, propriety, rightness in this course of action; it is in line, on-target, tending toward the service and glory of God. There is a goodness about it; it contributes to a closer union with God. In a letter to Theresa Rajadell in 1536, Ignatius wrote about this particular point: "It remains for me to speak how we ought to understand what we think is from the Lord, and, understanding it, how we ought to use it for our advantage. For it frequently happens that Our Lord moves and urges the soul to this or that activity. He begins by enlightening the soul; that is to say, by speaking interiorly to it without the din of words, without any possibility of resistance on our part, even should we wish to resist."[48] Ignatius seems to be describing here what he calls consolation without a cause.

Another possibility is the consolation with a known cause, such as good or pious thoughts. This consolation can come from either the good or evil spirit. To discern the spirit, Ignatius advises individuals to review the whole course of their thoughts;

if they begin good and end in something evil, distracting, or less good, the consolation is the work of the evil spirit who began by assuming the appearance of goodness. The judgment here, where causes can be identified, is something of an application of the principle "by their fruits you shall know them." Where no cause is discernible, the consolation must be from God.

Before we leave this matter of how to discover the will of God in a particular concrete choice, it will be important to consider certain recent theological thinking about the will of God itself. Is the will of God a prearranged plan in the divine mind (let us say B), so that as I choose among alternate goods A, B, and C, if I choose A, I might actually be missing the will of God for me? Or is the crucial part of finding God's will in the process itself and not in the thing chosen? Could finding God's will be not so much choosing the right object but simply in choosing for God? Perhaps the will of God will coincide with whatever good I choose, providing I am truly seeking God and not simply myself in the choosing.

As we move away from a static, structured view of the world and ourselves, and begin to see things in process and evolution, we are getting away from the notion that there may be some blueprint in the mind of God that we might discover if we follow the right procedure. There is really no will of God in this sense. God's will for the world and for people is bound up with his creative act, his divine knowledge and support of the creative processes in the world and particularly in the creativity of mankind. Says one theologian,

> It is in this context that human decision-making is really, if you want, the process of determining the will of God.

> This is what God is doing—He is sustaining creatively this process by which human beings, with several options before them, and in many cases options which are relatively neutral, any one of which might be a good choice—they are the cutting-edge of what you might call the Will of God. That is why we are here. We human beings are meant to shape the development of history and the development of evolution, even of the cosmos itself, from this point onward.[49]

This is a contemporary view. We cannot say that Ignatius had this view of the world and of God's will, but we can say that his method for decision making based on the discernment of spirits is congruent and compatible with this view. For as a person ponders or considers a certain good course of action, the feeling of consolation they experience comes from God alone. They will feel peace, joy, and rightness of choice only if they are truly choosing for God. Whatever the particular concrete choice they make in this context, it can be said to be the will of God no matter what its specific content may be. What Ignatius proposes is a methodology for choosing that places the emphasis not on the concrete particularities of the choices but on the conditions and context out of which the choice is made. Once again, what is chosen is not so important as that the choice be made in faith, in grace, in love, and for the service of God. It is the dispositions, the intentions, and the motives that are most important. These were Ignatius's primary concerns.

Spirituality for Our Time

Are the essential elements of traditional spirituality viable in an active apostolic life today? Can we find a solid spirituality operative in the life of a person who is deeply attuned to our own times? We can find just this in the life and writings of Pierre Teilhard de Chardin, S.J. His worldview is at once contemporary and profoundly spiritual. It is contemporary because it is evolutionary, seeing the world in process. It is spiritual because his is a faith-vision of the world and of man.

Teilhard de Chardin (1881–1955) was a French Jesuit priest and a world-renowned paleontologist whose spiritual writings were published and translated after his death. Teilhard has profoundly influenced our time and has caught the fancy of hundreds of thousands of people, believers and nonbelievers alike. We will sketch in barest outline Teilhard's faith-vision of the world, and then describe his spirituality, a finding God in all things, which follows upon this vision.

The fundamental premise in Teilhard's vision is that the world is in process; it is in a state of becoming; it is in evolution. "To our clearer vision the universe is no longer a State but a Process. The cosmos has become a Cosmogenesis."[50]

"Cosmogenesis" is Teilhard's own term for the ordered whole of the world in the process of becoming. The world is developing, moving from the stages of prelife to life, toward the perfection of human thought and knowledge and unanimity. This changed notion of the world, from something static to something in process, is fundamental for the understanding of our times.

In his major work, *The Phenomenon of Man,* Teilhard begins with the phenomenon of biology. This reveals biogenesis—an emerging process in the world of living things, a biological development that advances toward consciousness. Teilhard sees a line of progress developing toward consciousness—the power of a living thing to know, to sense, and to be aware of the world around it. This rise of increasing consciousness marks the axis of evolution. As biogenesis develops, it reaches a point where consciousness appears—in human beings.

Complexification and convergence are two dynamic principles that emerge in this process of evolution as Teilhard observed it. Complexification is the multiplication of molecules and cells in organisms as their consciousness increases. Psychic energy increases with the complexity of organized units. The second principle is that of convergence—the gathering of elements or units together into an organized and unified pattern. This is not only multiplication of units but also their coming together and interacting with one another.

The phenomenon of mankind begins at the threshold of reflection. When consciousness becomes self-consciousness, when biogenesis develops to the point where consciousness reflects upon itself, the phenomenon of mankind appears. Man not only knows, but knows that he knows. With the emergence of mankind, of reflex consciousness in the world, a new kind of growth appears, that of human knowledge and personality. The world is enveloped with another sphere, another layer of life, the noosphere—the sphere of knowledge and the growth of science. This growth and development of science Teilhard calls *noogenesis* from the Greek word *nous,* "mind," and *genesis,* "the process of becoming." Noogenesis describes the evolution of man, his growth in consciousness and knowledge.

The principles that foster human growth and development (hominization) are the same ones that Teilhard discovered operating in biological evolution: complexity and convergence. Complexification is the increasing world population—more and more human beings, more centers of consciousness, greater human development. Convergence is the physical and psychic interaction of people, communication, socialization. The very roundness of the world itself guarantees and contributes to this convergence of persons.

Although people will multiply and increase regularly, their social convergence is not fully guaranteed. The counterdynamics that jeopardize the process of human unification are selfishness, isolationism, divisiveness, egocentricity, war, and in the Christian context, sin. Human freedom creates these possibilities that endanger the whole evolutionary process and render its ultimate success doubtful and insecure.

What then is the human ultimate? Teilhard calls this the Omega point. He projects his basic vision into the future and sees a supreme act of collective vision. He sees indications of this in the scientific explosion and the great increase of knowledge in our world. He projects his vision of human convergence to what he terms a "megasynthesis," a great synthesis of all human beings. This socialization is gradually taking place, for instance, in a metropolis where many people come together and interact. The city is the spearhead of evolution and progress, the center of modern life.

Teilhard's appendix to *The Phenomenon of Man* is called "The Christian Phenomenon" and here he turns from scientific data and hypothetical projection to the data of Christian revelation. Here the end of all process and all evolution is already given. Omega already exists and is operative at the core of all being. Teilhard says it radiates from one center to all centers personally. In other words, the whole dynamic evolution of the world is the result of the attractive force of the Omega point who is God himself supporting, energizing, and working in this whole process. He is present and working in the world according to the principles of complexification and convergence.

Teilhard finds the presence of God in the world and throughout the world. He develops this aspect of his vision in his book *The Divine Milieu.* Here is a profoundly faith-oriented vision of the world and of God the Alpha and Omega of all creation. God created the world, or better, *creates the world;* for Teilhard's notion of creation is not the making of a static world but that of continuous creation in which God works constantly through complexification and convergence to bring the world ever closer to perfection and to himself.

The ongoing creation of the cosmos is for Teilhard a progressive cosmogenesis, biogenesis, noogenesis, and ultimately Christogenesis, in which each process prepares for and leads to and supports the next one. And because God supports and works throughout the whole series, he is everywhere, omnipresent, a divine milieu.

Teilhard finds God at the very source of human life and the source of all that happens to people in the world. God is present in all that influences a person both from within and without.

Teilhard even finds God working in the diminishments of suffering and of death: "When I feel I am losing hold of myself and am absolutely passive within the hands of the great unknown forces that have formed me, in all these dark moments, O God, grant that I may understand that it is You, provided only my faith is strong enough, who are painfully parting the fibers of my being in order to penetrate to the very marrow of my substance and bear me away within yourself."[51]

The crowning instance of the presence of God in the world is the incarnation of Jesus Christ. In him, God enters the world in a special, historical way and assumes dynamic leadership of all of cosmic evolution. Teilhard's notion of redemption follows the principles of biological evolution and development. At the divine inbreak of Christ, God immerses himself and identifies himself with the whole process of evolution. He ultimately redeems people and the world by uniting them to himself organically in Christ Jesus. In the Pauline sense, people are redeemed by a physical incorporation into the Body of Christ. Through him and with him and in him all are returned to the Father.

The process of redemption in Christ Jesus is also a process of unification of people, the ultimate instance of convergence of people in love. It is Christ who by his life and by his grace energizes this same dynamic of convergence and guarantees its ultimate success and perfection.

The chief instrument through which Christ energizes and unifies the faithful within himself is the Eucharist. Teilhard's notion of the Eucharist is not simply that it is formed and communicated to persons but that it pervades and permeates those who receive it and through them it comes into contact with the whole material world. This is the expansion of the Host, which penetrates the whole of creation. From this permeation of the hearts of people and of the world, Christ draws all to himself. "Christ Jesus, who through the magnetism of his love and the effective power of his Eucharist, gradually gathers into himself all the unitive energy scattered through his creation."[52] With St. Paul, Teilhard would say to the Christians, "All things are yours, and you are Christ's, and Christ is God's."

What will the consummation of this process be? What will the second coming of Christ be all about? Teilhard asks whether the world has two summits of fulfillment or only one. In other words, does the world have a natural end and a supernatural end too? His answer is no: "The world can no more have two summits of fulfillment than a circumference can have two centers."[53] To build the earth is to prepare for and to hasten the second coming of Christ. Christ has entered this whole dynamic of the human world by his Incarnation and leads the whole process to his heavenly Father where God will be all in all. All the processes within the world will be assumed by Christ and led to the Father. Teilhard writes, "In a universe which was disclosing itself to me as structurally convergent, you, Lord Jesus, by right of your resurrection had assumed the dominating position of all-inclusive Center in which everything is gathered together."[54]

Teilhard sees the evolving universe focused into a single redeeming and elevating process. All things will be united to Christ and will find their fulfillment in him. There will be a new heaven and a new earth when Christ reestablishes all things in himself and finally returns all to his Father.

This has been a sketch of Teilhard's faith-vision of God, people, and the world. It is the basis for his Ignatian spirituality of finding God in all things.

To summarize the implications of this vision, we might distinguish four aspects of the spiritual life that can be components for an apostolic Christian life in our time.

The first aspect is a Christian outlook—a faith-vision of the world. This is the way individuals see things, the way they interpret their experience. In moments of reflection or writing or serious conversation individuals may articulate their vision of the world. For a Christian this vision will be a faith-vision. The way a person understands God, people, and the world will have a profound influence on their whole spirituality.

The second aspect of any spirituality must be a finding or seeking of God in formal prayer. This is raising the heart and mind to God in meditation, contemplation, and liturgical prayer. It is an interior exercise of prayer, which we saw for Ignatius was not an end but a means in the spiritual life. It can be used to foster and enrich one's faith-vision. It may be a means for finding God's will, a time for discernment, and it is ordered to the service of God and action for the kingdom of Christ. We meet this sort of prayer in the Spiritual Exercises of

Ignatius. We also find this type of prayerful expression throughout the writings of Teilhard: "But for these moments of more efficient or more explicit contact, the tide of the divine omnipresence and our perception of it would weaken until all that was best in our human endeavor, without being entirely lost to the world, would be emptied of God."[55]

A third aspect of the spiritual life is finding God in activity. This is prayer as a style of life in God's service. To find God's will is to find God, and to do God's will is to be united with God. Teilhard writes, "Let us ponder over this basic truth till we are steeped in it. God at his most vitally active and most incarnate is not remote from us, wholly apart from the sphere of the tangible. On the contrary, at every moment he awaits us in the activity, in the work to be done which every moment brings."[56] Total active dedication to God's will in a spirit of loving obedience will presuppose and actually involve a thoroughgoing asceticism, a self-denial geared to service, and constant mortification.

The fourth and last aspect of a spirituality is finding God in an experiential awareness of the presence of God. This is a sense or perception of God's operative presence in the world or in oneself. It is a gift, a special grace; it is the perfection of faith, and at its highest levels it is mysticism. Teilhard once wrote, "Lord Jesus, when it was given to me to see where the dazzling trail of particular beauties and partial harmonies was leading, I recognized that it was all coming to a center on a single point, a single person, yourself. Every presence makes me feel that you are near me, every touch is the touch of your hand, every necessity transmits to me a pulsation of your will."[57]

With Teilhard we might pray, "Lord grant that I may see, that I may see you, that I may see and experience you present and animating all things. . . . Jesus, help me to perfect the perception and expression of my vision. . . . Help me to the right action, the right word, help me to give the example that will reveal you best."[58]

Notes

1. Pierre Teilhard de Chardin, S.J., *The Future of Man* (New York: Harper & Row, 1964), 12.

2. Quoted in Christopher F. Mooney, S.J., "Ignatian Spirituality and Modern Theology," *Downside Review* 80 (1962): 334.

3. St. Athanasius, *Life of Anthony,* chap. xiv.

4. Pelagius the Deacon, *Verba Seniorum,* xvii, 5.

5. Hubert Van Zeller, *The Benedictine Ideal* (London: Burns & Oates, 1959), 2.

6. Elmer O'Brien, "On Prayer, #17," in *Varieties of Mystic Experience,* (New York: Holt, Rinehart and Winston, 1964), 61.

7. Ibid., #18, 61.

8. Ibid., #61, 62.

9. Ibid., #57, 62.

10. Ibid., #142, 63.

11. Benedictine Monks of St. Meinrad, *The Holy Rule of St. Benedict* (St. Meinrad, IN: Grail Press, 1956), vii.

12. Van Zeller, *Benedictine Idea.*

13. Meinrad, *The Holy Rule,* 85.

14. Ibid., 78.

15. Gerard Sitwell, O.S.B., *Spiritual Writers of the Middle Ages* (New York: Hawthorn Books, 1961), 21.

16. Ronald Knox, *Enthusiasm* (Oxford: Clarendon Press, 1950), 71–89.

17. Quoted in Josef Pieper, *Guide to Thomas Aquinas* (New York: Pantheon, 1962), 23.

18. Quoted in Herbert B. Workman, *The Evolution of the Monastic Ideal* (Boston: Beacon Press, 1962), 272.

19. *Little Flowers of St. Francis,* chap. xvi.

20. Thomas à Kempis, *The Imitation of Christ.* I, xix.

21. Ibid., I, x.

22. Thomas Aquinas, *Summa Theologiae.* II–II, 9. 188, a. 6.

23. Johan Huizinga, *Waning of the Middle Ages* (London: Edward Arnold, 1924), 1.

24. "Of the most powerful Prayer of all," *The Talks of Instruction.*

25. Huizinga, *Waning of the Middle Ages,* 203.

26. Ibid.

27. O'Brien, *Varieties of Mystic Experience,* 151.

28. Huizinga, *Waning of the Middle Ages,* 136–37.

29. Karl Rahner, S.J., *Visions and Prophesies* (New York: Herder and Herder, 1963), 17.

30. *Spiritual Exercises,* #236.

31. Jean Danielou, S.J., "The Ignatian Vision of the Universe and of Man," *Cross Currents* 4 (1954): 364.

32. *Epistola Ignatiana,* VI, 91. Quoted in Maurice Giuliani, *Finding God in All Things,* trans. by William J. Young, S.J. (Chicago: Henry Regnery Co., 1958), 17.

33. Ibid., II.

34. Ibid., 22–23.

35. Ibid., 8–9.

36. Danielou, "Ignatian Vision."

37. Ibid., 366.

38. Hermann Tuchle, "Baroque Christianity: The Root of Triumphalism?" in *Historical Problems of Church Renewal,* ed. Roger Aubert (Glen Rock, NJ: Paulist, 1965), 138–40.

39. *Constitutions,* part VI, chap. iii, 1.

40. *Scripta de S. Ignatio,* I, 515.

41. *Epistolae P. Hieronymi Nadal,* II, 32.

42. Quoted in P. Leturia, S.J., "De oratione matutina in Societate Iesu documenta selecta," *Archivum Historicum S.J.* III (1934): 102.

43. Heinrich Schlier, *Principalities and Powers in the New Testament* (New York: Herder and Herder, 1961).

44. Quoted in *Existentialism from Dostoevsky to Sartre,* ed. Walter Kaufman (New York: Meridian Books, 1963), 287–311.

45. *Spiritual Exercises,* #176.

46. Ibid., #338.

47. Ibid.

48. William J. Young, S.J., trans., *Letters of St. Ignatius Loyola* (Chicago: Loyola University Press, 1959), 22.

49. Bernard Cooke, S.J. (unpublished proceedings, Santa Clara Conference on Total Jesuit Formation, 1967, III, Pt. 2, p. 162).

50. Pierre Teilhard de Chardin, S.J., *The Future of Man,* 261.

51. Pierre Teilhard de Chardin, S.J., *The Divine Milieu* (New York: Harper and Brothers, 1960), 62.

52. Pierre Teilhard de Chardin, S.J., *Hymn of the Universe* (New York: Harper & Row, 1965), 119.

53. Ibid., 149.

54. Ibid., 151.

55. Teilhard de Chardin, S.J., *Divine Milieu,* 35.

56. Teilhard de Chardin, S.J., *Hymn of the Universe,* 83–84.

57. Ibid., 153.